Say It, S

The Self-Esteem Affirmation Activity Journal
for Girls And Their Mothers

Say It, See It, Believe It

The Self-Esteem Affirmation Activity Journal for Girls And Their Mothers

Published by: Strategies for Empowered Living Inc

Contents

Intro

How would you like to feel more confident on the inside and build the kind of self-esteem that will keep you feeling positive toward yourself no matter what challenges come your way? Well, it's possible if you learn how to make your words work for you. Believe it or not, your words have a lot of power. Your words have the power to build you up, and your words have the power to discourage you, depending on how you use them. This is why it is so important that you learn how to use your words to build high self-esteem and develop a positive outlook on life.

Say It See It Believe It is an affirmation activity journal for you to read with your mom. It will show you how to use the power of your words to think bigger, recognize your value and dream beyond any limits that others have placed on you or that you have placed on yourself. What's more, it will show your mom as well as any other caregivers in your life how to support you in building healthy self-esteem and inner resilience.

So what are affirmations? Simply put, affirmations are positive statements designed to help you do three things:
1. Think and act more positively toward yourself.

2. Instill calm during stressful times.
3. Activate your mind to pump you up with so much positive motivation and inner confidence that you actually begin to believe the best about yourself and as a result start taking steps in the direction of your desired outcomes.

Why should you read this book with your mother? Because the more support that you have in building your self-confidence and inner resilience from people who truly care about you, the more you'll realize how special and valuable you are and that you have what it takes to succeed in life.

What if your mom is not around? Then read and do the affirmation activity journal with a concerned caregiver who wants the best for you or a person whom you look to as a mother-figure.

Say It See It Believe It contains four sections:

1.) <u>The Affirmation</u> – this is the positive statement that you are going to say to yourself as many times as you need to say it until you pump yourself up with so much positive self-talk that you actually begin to believe it and act on it.

2.) <u>Why It Works</u> – this explains how the affirmation will benefit you.

3.) <u>Memos for Moms</u> – these are tips to help your mother or caregiver support you in building stronger self-confidence and resilience.

4.) <u>Journal Space</u> - this is exactly what it sounds like...a space where you can write about anything you want. You can write a song, poem, what you think about each affirmation. You can place stickers in this section or anything else that you desire.

Also included in this book are activities for mothers and daughters to do together.

Say It See It Believe It will show you how to use the power of positive self-affirmation to help you develop a winning mindset so that you can become a more positive, empowered you.

I'll be rooting for you,

Cassandra Mack

1

I Like Myself

☆Why This Affirmation Works☆
...Liking yourself is the first step toward building positive self-esteem. When you like yourself, you start to appreciate your own unique qualities and all of the special things that you have to offer.

Memos for Moms

☺ Accept your daughter for who she is, not who you want her to be. If you can accept your daughter just the way she is, you will provide her with the core building blocks for developing healthy self-esteem and strong confidence.

☺ Value your daughter's uniqueness.

☺ Tell your daughter one thing that you like about her for seven days in a row.

❀ Journal Space ❀

_____

_____

_____

_____

_____

_____

_____

_____

_____

_____

_____

_____

_____

_____

_____

_____

_____

_____

_____

_____

_____

_____

_____

_____

_____

_____

_____

_____

_____

_____

_____

_____

_____

_____

_____

_____

_____

_____

_____

_____

_____

_____

_____

_____

_____

_____

2.

I Respect Myself.

☆Why This Affirmation Works☆
...When you respect yourself you increase your feelings of self-worth. When you respect yourself, you make respectable choices that you can feel good about long term. When you respect yourself, you set the standard for how other people will treat you. When you respect yourself you also treat others with the same level of respect that you would like to be treated with.

Memos for Moms

☺ Define the word respect for your daughter. Give her examples of how to speak with respect, treat others with respect, carry herself respectably and make decisions that lead to increased feelings of self-respect.

☺ Ask your daughter to give you more examples of ways that she can respect herself.

☺ Model the characteristic of self-respect by being an example of excellence and integrity.

❀ Journal Space ❀

_____

_____

_____

_____

_____

_____

_____

_____

_____

_____

_____

_____

_____

_____

_____

_____

_____

_____

_____

_____

_____

_____

_____

_____

_____

_____

_____

_____

_____

_____

_____

_____

_____

_____

_____

_____

_____

_____

_____

_____

_____

_____

_____

_____

_____

_____

3.

I Am Accomplishing
New Things Every Day

☆Why This Affirmation Works☆

...We all need to feel proud of ourselves. Recognizing your accomplishments both big and small enables you to feel proud of yourself. It also gives you the confidence to take on new challenges.

Memos for Moms

☺ Catch your daughter doing something right and praise her for it.

☺ Let your daughter know that you are proud of her.

☺ Help your daughter recognize her accomplishments both big and small.

❀ Journal Space ❀

_____

_____

_____

_____

_____

_____

_____

_____

_____

_____

_____

_____

_____

_____

_____

_____

_____

_____

_____

_____

_____

_____

_____

_____

_____

_____

_____

_____

_____

_____

_____

_____

_____

_____

_____

_____

_____

_____

_____

_____

_____

_____

_____

_____

_____

_____

4.

I Love Myself Through Thick and Thin

☆Why This Affirmation Works☆

...We all need to learn how to love ourselves unconditionally, no matter what happens to us in life and no matter what other people may think about us. When you learn to love yourself through thick and thin, you begin to realize how special and valuable you are. When you love yourself unconditionally, you learn to accept yourself just the way you are while striving to become the best person that you can be.

Memos for Moms

☺ Let your daughter know that she is loved and lovable no matter what.

☺ Tell your daughter that you love her every day.

☺ Show your daughter physical expressions of love like hugs and kisses or a pat on the back.

❀ Journal Space ❀

_____

_____

_____

_____

_____

_____

_____

_____

_____

_____

_____

_____

_____

_____

_____

_____

_____

_____

_____

_____

_____

_____

_____

_____

_____

_____

_____

_____

_____

_____

_____

_____

_____

_____

_____

_____

_____

_____

_____

_____

_____

_____

_____

_____

5.

There Is So Much More To Me Than The Way I Look

☆Why This Affirmation Works☆

...We all need to learn to look deeper than our facial features, our skin tone, our hair, our weight, our dress size and our body type. When you look deeper than your looks, you discover the real you.

Memos for Moms

☺ Let your daughter know that there are more important things in life than the way we look.

☺ Tell your daughter often that she is beautiful and special on the inside and on the outside.

☺ Remind your daughter that pretty is as pretty does: ...Meaning that when a person is mean and insensitive toward others it makes them less attractive on the outside no matter what they look like.

❀ Journal Space ❀

_____

_____

_____

_____

_____

_____

_____

_____

_____

_____

_____

_____

_____

_____

_____

_____

_____

_____

_____

_____

_____

_____

_____

_____

_____

_____

_____

_____

_____

_____

_____

_____

_____

_____

_____

_____

_____

_____

_____

_____

_____

_____

_____

_____

_____

_____

_____

_____

6.

I Create My Own Style and I Like It

☆Why This Affirmation Works☆

...When you learn to create your own style instead of blindly following every new fashion trend, you'll be surprised at how quickly you discover your own fashion sense. You'll also discover that having your own sense of style means that you are confident enough to do your own thing even if it's a little different from the other girls. Plus, you'll become very creative and learn that you can look great without having to spend a lot of money on clothes.

Memos for Moms

☺ Encourage your daughter to discover her own fashion sense.

☺ Help your daughter learn how to dress appropriate for her age and body type. Always remember that a closely-fitted sweater gives off a different look on a 44 double D cup than it does on a 32-A. So depending on your daughter's body frame you may have to show her how to wear the same styles as her peers in ways that are appropriate for her body and that do not draw attention that she is not prepared to handle.

☺ Help your daughter realize that she can dress trendy without being revealing.

❀ Journal Space ❀

_____

_____

_____

_____

_____

_____

_____

_____

_____

_____

_____

_____

_____

_____

_____

_____

_____

_____

_____

_____

_____

_____

_____

_____

_____

_____

_____

_____

_____

_____

_____

_____

_____

_____

_____

_____

_____

_____

_____

_____

_____

_____

_____

_____

_____

_____

_____

_____

7.

I Speak Up for Myself

☆Why This Affirmation Works☆
...Speaking up for yourself is how you set boundaries, advocate for yourself and express what's on your mind.

Memos for Moms

☺ Encourage your daughter to speak up for herself.

☺ Role-play different situations that might call for your daughter to speak up for herself.

☺ Talk to your daughter about the importance of setting boundaries and expressing her needs and desires.

❀ Journal Space ❀

_____

_____

_____

_____

_____

_____

_____

_____

_____

_____

_____

_____

_____

_____

_____

_____

_____

_____

_____

_____

_____

_____

_____

_____

_____

8.

I Am Making Better Choices Each Day

☆Why This Affirmation Works☆

...Striving to make good choices gives you a sense of personal control and empowerment. It also builds leadership skills.

Memos for Moms

☺ Talk to your daughter about the importance of making good choices.

☺ Explain to your daughter that our values guide every choice we make. Let her know that the clearer we are about our values, the easier it becomes to make good choices.

☺ Help your daughter come up with ways to stay true to her values when she's faced with tough choices. Give examples of tough choice situations. Ask her to share how she might respond if she was faced with a tough choice that went against her values.

❀ Journal Space ❀

_____

_____

_____

_____

_____

_____

_____

_____

_____

_____

_____

_____

_____

_____

_____

_____

_____

_____

_____

_____

_____

_____

_____

9.

I Am A Positive Thinker

☆Why This Affirmation Works☆

...Our thoughts determine our outlook in life and how much effort we put into our plans and dreams. When you think positively you improve your attitude and make better choices. Not only that, when obstacles come your way instead of being defeated by them you will think of creative ways to work around or overcome them.

Memos for Moms

☺ Be positive toward your daughter. Speak positive words into her life. Let her know that you think the world of her, especially when she's feeling discouraged.

☺ When a situation looks bleak, try to encourage your daughter to look on the bright side.

☺ Get an index card or post-it and write down at least three strengths that your daughter possesses. Tomorrow at breakfast, leave the index card or post-it near her breakfast plate or bowl.

❀ Journal Space ❀

_____

_____

_____

_____

_____

_____

_____

_____

_____

_____

_____

_____

_____

_____

_____

_____

_____

_____

_____

_____

_____

_____

10.

I Can Make Friends Naturally and Easily

☆Why This Affirmation Works☆

...Acknowledging that you have what it takes to make friends naturally, allows you to meet new people with greater ease. Even more, it helps you build positive friendships with other young people who you share things in common with.

Memos for Moms

☺ Encourage your daughter to be open to meeting new friends.

☺ Encourage your daughter to join different clubs and activities in order to meet new and diverse kinds of people.

☺ Encourage your daughter to embrace diversity.

❀ Journal Space ❀

_____

_____

_____

_____

_____

_____

_____

_____

_____

_____

_____

_____

_____

_____

_____

_____

_____

_____

_____

_____

_____

_____

_____

_____

_____

_____

_____

_____

_____

_____

_____

_____

_____

_____

_____

_____

_____

_____

_____

_____

_____

_____

_____

_____

_____

_____

11.

I Help Other Girls Feel Included

☆Why This Affirmation Works☆

...Helping another girl feel included is how you make new friends and build stronger bonds with the friends you already have. It also demonstrates empathy and kindness since nobody likes to feel left out.

Memos for Moms

☺ Think back to when you were in middle or high school. Were you ever made to feel left out? If the answer is yes, then you know that it is not a good feeling. Help your daughter understand the importance of being inclusive toward other girls instead of excluding them.

☺ Help your daughter develop empathy toward others.

☺ Tell your daughter to make an effort to say hello to the new girl or invite a girl who always eats lunch by herself over to her table. Help her to remember that kindness goes a long way.

❀ Journal Space ❀

_____

_____

_____

_____

_____

_____

_____

_____

_____

_____

_____

_____

_____

_____

_____

_____

_____

_____

_____

_____

_____

_____

12.

I Am Growing Stronger and Smarter Each Day

☆Why This Affirmation Works☆

...We naturally feel better about ourselves when we focus on our strengths and positive growth. Focusing on the ways that you are growing stronger and smarter motivates you to study harder and apply yourself more in the areas where you need to apply yourself.

Memos for Moms

☺ Encourage your daughter to focus on the ways that she is getting stronger and growing as a person.

☺ Point out your daughter's strengths. Name them one by one.

☺ Leave a Post-it note on her bed or mirror acknowledging at least one way that she has grown this year.

❀ Journal Space ❀

_____

_____

_____

_____

_____

_____

_____

_____

_____

_____

_____

_____

_____

_____

_____

_____

_____

_____

_____

_____

_____

_____

_____

_____

_____

_____

_____

_____

_____

_____

_____

_____

_____

_____

_____

_____

_____

_____

_____

_____

_____

_____

_____

_____

_____

_____

13.

I Love My Hair

☆Why This Affirmation Works☆

...Many girls and women have a love/hate relationship with their hair. When we acknowledge that all hair is good hair provided it is healthy, we are better able to love our hair and love ourselves from head to toe.

Memos for Moms

☺ There is no such thing as good hair. If it is on your head it's good. Help your daughter reject the notion of good hair, if your hair is healthy no matter the texture or style then it is good hair.

☺ Help your daughter think in terms of healthy hair instead of good and bad hair. Help her find hair care products that are uniquely designed for her hair.

☺ Show your daughter examples of other girls and women who look like her so that she can begin to realize that beauty comes in all skin tones, body types and hair textures.

❀ Journal Space ❀

_____

_____

_____

_____

_____

_____

_____

_____

_____

_____

_____

_____

_____

_____

_____

_____

_____

_____

_____

_____

_____

_____

_____

14.

My Skin Is Beautiful

☆Why This Affirmation Works☆

...Loving the skin you are in is an essential part of developing high self-esteem. This is the beginning of a healthy self-image.

Memos for Moms

☺ For many girls, particularly girls of color it can be a struggle to love the skin that they are in because often darker skin is not celebrated in fashion magazines and popular media. Help your daughter recognize that diverse skin tones are what makes each of us unique and beautiful in our own way.

☺ Help your daughter find realistic beauty role models that are representative of her skin tone, hair texture and size so that she can see images of beauty that look like her.

☺ Do an activity together where you and your daughter create a collage of girls and women from various magazines that celebrate diverse beauty.

❀ Journal Space ❀

_____

_____

_____

_____

_____

_____

_____

_____

_____

_____

_____

_____

_____

_____

_____

_____

_____

_____

_____

_____

_____

_____

_____

_____

_____

_____

_____

_____

_____

_____

_____

_____

_____

_____

_____

_____

_____

_____

_____

_____

_____

_____

_____

_____

_____

_____

_____

15.

I Complete My Class Assignments and All Homework On Time

☆Why This Affirmation Works☆

...When you complete your homework and class assignments on time, you get better grades. When you get good grades you feel smarter and more confident. When you excel in school you tend to have more options later on in life.

Memos for Moms

☺ Help your daughter to develop good homework habits such as: completing all assignments on time, asking for clear directions if there is something that she does not understand and pairing up with other classmates in order to study together.

☺ Stay abreast of your daughter's academic progress by staying in communication with her teachers and attending parent meetings.

☺ Stress the importance of reading for pleasure. Let your daughter know that readers are leaders. Better yet, start your own mother and daughter reading group and invite other mothers and daughters to join you.

❀ Journal Space ❀

_____

_____

_____

_____

_____

_____

_____

_____

_____

_____

_____

_____

_____

_____

_____

_____

_____

_____

_____

_____

_____

_____

_____

_____

_____

_____

_____

_____

_____

_____

_____

_____

_____

_____

_____

_____

_____

_____

_____

_____

_____

_____

_____

_____

_____

16.

I Have A Bright Future

☆Why This Affirmation Works☆

...Having a sense of hope for the future encourages us to dream, make plans and set goals for the future.

Memos for Moms

☺ Encourage your daughter to dream. Be her biggest cheerleader by encouraging her to pursue her dreams.

☺ Remind your daughter that every great feat, every great achievement and every great accomplishment started out as a dream in somebody's mind.

☺ Be the inspiration that your daughter needs by pursuing your own dreams.

❀ Journal Space ❀

_____

_____

_____

_____

_____

_____

_____

_____

_____

_____

_____

_____

_____

_____

_____

_____

_____

_____

_____

_____

_____

_____

_____

_____

_____

_____

_____

_____

_____

_____

_____

_____

_____

_____

_____

_____

_____

_____

_____

_____

_____

_____

_____

_____

_____

_____

17.

I Am Intelligent and I Am Not Afraid To Show It

☆Why This Affirmation Works☆
...Acknowledging your intelligence helps you realize that you have the ability to learn anything and achieve just about any goal, even a difficult one, as long as you give it 100% effort.

Memos for Moms

☺ Nurture your daughter's intelligence. Keep track of the subjects that she excels at and the subjects that she need to put more effort in. Get her the support she needs to succeed in school.

☺ Explain to your daughter that intelligence comes in many forms like: common sense, good judgment, empathy, leadership abilities and so on.

☺ Encourage your daughter to read the book, "You're Smarter Than You Think: A Kid's Guide to Multiple Intelligences," by Thomas Armstrong. Even better...read it with her.

❀ Journal Space ❀

_____

_____

_____

_____

_____

_____

_____

_____

_____

_____

_____

_____

_____

_____

_____

_____

_____

_____

_____

_____

_____

_____

18.

I Can Do Whatever I Set My Mind To

☆Why This Affirmation Works☆

...Knowing that you can do virtually anything that you set your mind to will motivate you to keep trying when faced with things that are difficult or challenging.

Memos for Moms

☺ Be vigilant about helping your daughter understand the importance of persistence, especially when it comes to her education and the pursuit of her goals.

☺ If your daughter says she cannot do something, ask her why she feels that way. Suggests additional ways for her to think about how to tackle the challenge.

☺ Encourage your daughter to play checkers or chess. It will develop her critical thinking skills. Better yet, start a tradition of family game night where the two of you and or other family members play board games together.

❀ Journal Space ❀

_____

_____

_____

_____

_____

_____

_____

_____

_____

_____

_____

_____

_____

_____

_____

_____

_____

_____

_____

_____

_____

19.

I Believe In Myself

☆Why This Affirmation Works☆

...When you believe in yourself you become a powerhouse of possibility able to achieve great things. When you believe in yourself you will refuse to allow other people to talk you out of pursuing your goals and dreams.

Memos for Moms

☺ Show your daughter that you believe in her in ways that convince her.

☺ Trust your daughter to make good decisions. Trust that you taught her well.

☺ Give your daughter increased responsibility as she get older. Giving your daughter increased responsibility shows her that you trust and believe that she will do the right thing. However, at the same time remind your daughter that with increased responsibility comes increased accountability.

❀ Journal Space ❀

_____

_____

_____

_____

_____

_____

_____

_____

_____

_____

_____

_____

_____

_____

_____

_____

_____

_____

_____

_____

_____

_____

_____

20.

I Have A Great Personality

☆Why This Affirmation Works☆

...When you connect with the best part of yourself – the part of you that is kind, generous, considerate, trustworthy and pleasant to be around, you build better relationships faster. When you remind yourself that deep down inside you have a great personality, you will develop the positive characteristics that are necessary to become a great person who is pleasant to be around.

Memos for Moms

☺ Help your daughter understand the importance of being a good person with a pleasant personality. Many girls think that it's cool to give off a snotty attitude. Let your daughter know that in the long run being kind to others will always trump being cliquey and popular.

☺ Teach you daughter not to promote or engage in cliquey and hurtful behavior toward others.

☺ Reinforce your daughter's individuality so that she will have the strength to go against the crowd if need be.

❀ Journal Space ❀

_____

_____

_____

_____

_____

_____

_____

_____

_____

_____

_____

_____

_____

_____

_____

_____

_____

_____

_____

_____

21.

I Am Responsible

...This affirmation reminds you that you have the smarts and the power to behave responsibly by making good choices. It affirms that you can be trusted and counted on to do the right thing... regardless of what other people choose to do.

Memos for Moms

☺ Use choice to encourage responsible behavior. Choices can be given to your daughter to increase responsibility at home, which over time will increase her ability to behave responsibly when she is away from home.

☺ Help your daughter to understand that being responsible means more than just being "good." It also means that with every choice there is a consequence.

☺ Be clear and fair. In order to help your daughter behave more responsibly it's important that you set clear expectations and be fair and reasonable with her.

❀ Journal Space ❀

_____

_____

_____

_____

_____

_____

_____

_____

_____

_____

_____

_____

_____

_____

_____

_____

_____

_____

_____

_____

_____

_____

_____

_____

_____

_____

_____

_____

_____

_____

_____

_____

_____

_____

_____

_____

_____

_____

_____

_____

_____

_____

_____

22.

I Am Able To Solve Problems Creatively

☆Why This Affirmation Works☆

...This affirmation reminds you that with a little thought and creativity you can solve virtually any problem that comes your way. And if you cannot solve the problem, you can creatively learn to work around it.

Memos for Moms

☺ When your daughter asks you what you think about a situation, turn the question back to her and discuss the issue together. This builds her problem solving and critical thinking skills.

☺ Encourage your daughter to become an independent thinker. Schedule a regular current event night where during meal time you direct her attention to a current event either local or worldwide and ask her what she thinks about the issue.

☺ Encourage your daughter to voice her opinions. The more she's encouraged to speak up for herself the more she'll be able to solve problems creatively.

❀ Journal Space ❀

_____

_____

_____

_____

_____

_____

_____

_____

_____

_____

_____

_____

_____

_____

_____

_____

_____

_____

_____

_____

_____

_____

_____

_____

_____

_____

_____

_____

_____

_____

_____

_____

_____

_____

_____

_____

_____

_____

_____

_____

_____

_____

_____

_____

_____

_____

_____

23.

There Are People All Around Me Who Want Me To Succeed

☆Why This Affirmation Works☆

...When you know that there are people in your life who are rooting for you to win, you will be motivated to put your best foot forward.

Memos for Moms

☺ Let your daughter know as often as possible that you see great things in store for her. Give her specific examples.

☺ Show interest in the things that your daughter is interested in. If she writes poetry, ask her to recite one for you. If she likes to draw, frame one of her pictures and display it prominently on your wall.

☺ Show your daughter that you are impressed with her in ways that will inspire her to rise even higher.

❀ Journal Space ❀

_____

_____

_____

_____

_____

_____

_____

_____

_____

_____

_____

_____

_____

_____

_____

_____

_____

_____

_____

_____

_____

_____

_____

_____

_____

_____

_____

_____

_____

_____

_____

_____

_____

_____

_____

_____

_____

_____

_____

_____

_____

_____

_____

_____

_____

_____

24.
I Learn From My Mistakes

☆Why This Affirmation Works☆

...Everyone makes mistakes. Nobody's perfect. This affirmation reminds you that when you take the time to step back from the situation and learn from your mistakes you can do better the next time around. This affirmation also lets you know that you can use failure as a gauge for growth if you are willing to learn from your mistakes and commit to doing better next time.

Memos for Moms

☺ Let your daughter know that everybody makes mistakes. Remind her that what separates successful people from people who fail in life is the willingness to learn from our mistakes.

☺ When your daughter makes a mistake help her to think about what she can do differently next time around to improve her odds.

☺ Share some of the mistakes that you made when you were your daughter's age and what you learned from them.

❀ Journal Space ❀

_____

_____

_____

_____

_____

_____

_____

_____

_____

_____

_____

_____

_____

_____

_____

_____

_____

_____

_____

_____

_____

_____

25.
I Am Thankful for Everything I Have

☆Why This Affirmation Works☆

...Being thankful for everything you have, even if you do not have everything you want reminds you of the importance of being grateful and appreciative. It also helps you to remember to count your blessings because no matter how bad you think you have it there are other people all around the world who are worse off than you.

Memos for Moms

☺ Encourage your daughter to develop an attitude of gratitude.

☺ Many children and teens have an attitude of entitlement. Do not reinforce this type of attitude by passively giving your daughter everything she wants without making sure that she earns it. Nobody owes us anything. Instead, encourage your daughter to appreciate everything she has.

☺ Count your blessings. Teach your daughter to do the same.

❀ Journal Space ❀

_____

_____

_____

_____

_____

_____

_____

_____

_____

_____

_____

_____

_____

_____

_____

_____

_____

_____

_____

_____

_____

_____

_____
_____
_____
_____
_____
_____
_____
_____
_____
_____
_____
_____
_____
_____
_____
_____
_____
_____
_____
_____
_____
_____
_____
_____

Fun Activities for Mothers & Daughters

Activity #1.
Mother and Daughter Scrapbook

This activity is all about preserving treasured photos and memories. You'll need: a photo album, fabric, fabric glue, trimmings and your favorite photos. Dress up in your craziest, most creative outfits and take photos of one another. Then, make a scrapbook consisting of your favorite photos both old and new.

Activity #2.
Recipe Cards

This activity is all about passing on your favorite dishes and desserts as well as reminiscing on a favorite time with mom. Put together a collection of recipe cards, adding to each favorite dish a fun memory of a time with your mom and ask your mom to add a favorite time with her mom.

Activity #3
Alphabet Television Show

Starting with the letter "A" you and your mom take turns naming a television show that begins with each letter of the alphabet. For example for the letter "A" you might pick, "American Idol" or "All My Children" and so on. The first person who hesitates for too long is out. This is a wonderful way for mothers and daughters to learn about the television shows that were popular during each generation.

Activity #4
Guess Who I Am

Write down the name of a famous person and then pin the name on your mother's back. Make sure that she can't see the name that you have written. The object of the game is for her to try to figure out what name is on her back from the hints and clues that you will give her. Keep giving your mom hints and clues until she guesses the name that is on her back. Afterward, let your mom do the same thing to you.

Activity #5
I'm A Winner Poster

You and your mom are going to create your very own, I'm A Winner Poster that celebrates your collective gifts and talents. Then, you are going to top it off with a positive motto. For this activity you will need: a large sheet of paper, markers, colored pencils, paint, glue, glitter. Take out two sheets of paper both you and your mom write down five positive things you like about each other. Review these lists. Pulling from your lists, create a poster together that conveys how special you both are. Don't forget to cap your poster off with a great motto. Something positive that celebrates the mother and daughter bond.

Activity #6
Try Something New

For this activity you and your mom will need: assorted magazines, scissors, construction paper and a pen. Both you and your mom should cut out pictures of places you would like to go, things you would like to try and things that you would like to do one day in the future. You can cut out as many pictures as you like. Rate each item in priority order from the things you want to try, see and do right now to the things you want to try, see and do one day in the future. Select one picture from your pile. Glue it on a sheet of construction paper. At the bottom of the paper write today's date. Then set a date to try, see or do it. In your journal section write down what you imagine it would be like to try the new thing that you selected.

Activity #7
Take A Class Together

Taking a class together allows you and your mom to learn something new while spending quality time together. Plus, it gives you something to have in common to do as mother and daughter for years to come.

Activity #8
Get Fit Together

Get fit together. Find exercise activities that you can do together like taking a dance class, taking a morning walk together, bike riding or just encouraging each other to eat healthier and get more active. Focusing on health and fitness is an excellent way to spend quality time together as mother and daughter.

Activity #9
Music Video Critics

Tonight pretend that you and your mom are music video critics. Tell your mom that the two of you are going to do a critical review of your favorite music videos as well as some of the most popular videos that get the most air play. In the space below write down your top five music videos and how the girls and young women are dressed in them.

(Name of Video)   *(How Young Women Are Dressed)*

_____   _____

_____   _____

_____   _____

_____   _____

_____   _____

When you reflect on how the girls and young women dress and act in these videos, are the things you see and hear empowering to girls and young women or do they objectify girls and young women? Discuss your views with your mom.

Activity #10
How Well Do You Know Your Mother/Daughter

This activity is all about discovering new and unknown things about each other. Each of you can take turns writing down questions for the other to answer about each other, such as: "What is your mother's favorite song? What is your daughter's favorite commercial? What was your mother's favorite thing to wear when she was your age? What is the first thing that your daughter wants to do as soon as she gets home after school? ...and so on. Take turns answering questions about each other to see who knows the other the best.

Activity #11
Mother and Daughter High Tea

High Tea is a British custom that is fast becoming popular in the United States. A High Tea is a great event where you and your daughter can dress up in your Sunday best with hats, gloves and elegant party dresses for the daughters and cocktail or church dresses for the mothers, sip different teas and enjoy decadent desserts all while talking about anything you want and building etiquette skills. If you really want to go all out you can invest in a format tea set. If your budget is tight you can get creative using paper plates and cups and decorate them with fabric trimmings, motivational quotes and anything else that is festive and elegant. You can buy pastries or download your favorite dessert recipes and make them together. You can host a mother and daughter high tea and send out invitations to other mothers and daughters. You can also purchase plain teacups from a ceramics store and then paint the teacups making your own designs. It's your high tea, have fun with it.

Activity #12
Bake and Decorate Cookies Together

Download your favorite sugar cookie or ginger bread cookie recipe. Prepare the cookies according to the recipe directions. Set out bowls of tinted frosting and tubes of colored icing, along with decorative candies, and decorate your own cookies. You can also wrap them with colored cellophane paper and curling ribbon, place them in a decorative box and give them as gifts to others.

Activity #13
Mother/Daughter Manicures and Pedicures

Instead of spending money at the nail salon, give each other manicures and pedicures. This is a fun activity that both mother and daughter will enjoy. You can help each other choose colors for nail polish and create fun nail designs. You can buy nail art decals from any beauty supply store and add decals for extra pizzazz.

Activity #14
Five Questions About Life

Ask your daughter to write down 5 questions that she always wanted to know about life. Tell her she can ask anything at all. When she finishes, copy her questions down and ask her to answer them based on her own ideas and feelings. Once you have both finished answering the questions, swap papers, review at each other's answers and have a discussion around them over pizza.

Activity #15
Mother and Daughter Switch Day

Do you ever wish that you could make the rules for a day? Well then do the switch and be mom for a day. You get to make the rules provided it's nothing dangerous or too farfetched and your mom gets to be you. Here's the catch: You also have to get up early and assume the responsibilities of your mom like: waking everyone up, making breakfast, keeping track of everyone's schedule and so on. This activity allows daughters to walk in their mother's shoes and allows mother to see firsthand how their daughters view them.

Activity #16
Genealogy Activity

Sit down with your mom and research your genealogy. Find out who paved the way for your existence. Better yet, make a genealogy photo album with any photos, mementos or letters that you find. Go to websites like www.familysearch.org and www.genealogy.com to find out who and where you come from.

Activity #17
Three Achievements Activity

Each of you make a list of three things that you have achieved in your lives. It could be anything from passing a test, learning how to do something by yourself, etc.

Take turns sharing your list and congratulating each other. If you want to go all out, create certificates for one another on your computer and decorate them with stars, smiley faces and motivational stickers. Then present each other with certificates of achievement. This is a great way to build confidence and celebrate each other's achievements.

Activity #18
What To Wear Collage

Have you ever watched the show: "What Not To Wear? Well you are going to create a, What To Wear collage with your mother that illustrates age appropriate styles for both you and your mom. Grab a couple of your favorite fashion magazines, scissors and a photo album. You're going to create your very own Mother and Daughter style book. Look through the magazines and cut out pictures of the styles you like. However, there are the two rules to this activity: the styles must be age appropriate and it must be something that you would feel comfortable wearing. Each season you can update your style book with pictures of the new fashions but hook it up with your own personal flair.

Activity #19
Dream Collage

For this activity you'll need: magazines, newspapers, two pieces of poster board, two pair of scissors and glue. A good way for both you and your daughter to keep your dreams in front of you is to create a Dreams Collage. Think about some of the dreams that you have. Then, cut out words and pictures from the newspapers and magazines that represent some of your dreams. Glue your pictures to a piece of large poster board. Hang it up on your door or wall, so that you can keep your dreams in front of you.

Activity #20
Mother and Daughter Team Trivia

Invite five mothers and their daughters over for a game of Mother and Daughter Team Trivia. In this game mothers and their daughters are divided into mother and daughter teams. Each mother and daughter comes up with five questions for each other to answer that relate to the other. For example one question might be: "What will your mother say was the last excuse you gave to get out of cleaning your room?" Another example might be: What will your daughter say is the one thing that you complain about most often? How the game works is, first all of the mothers leave the room to answer the questions on a sheet of paper that their daughters came up with. Next the daughters leave the room to answer the questions on a sheet of paper that their mothers came up with. Then, the mothers and daughters come together to share their answers with the entire group. The mother and daughter team with the most correct answers wins.

Other Books By The Author

Cool, Confident and Strong: 52 Power Moves for Girls.

This book provides pre-teen and teenage girls with the tools they need to build self-esteem, deal with cliques and make decisions that respect their values, bodies and boundaries. Also included is a book discussion guide, tips for starting a Cool, Confident and Strong reading group and helpful websites for girls.

The Cool, Confident and Strong Self-Esteem and Smart Choices Workbook

This is the companion workbook to 'Cool, Confident and Strong; 52 Power Moves for Girls." It includes 52 reproducible activities that girls can complete on their own, that mothers can use with their daughters or that youth counselors and caregivers can use for a girls group.

Young Gifted and Doing It: 52 Power Moves for Teens

This success guide for teens provides 52 weekly strategies to help teens stay on the right track and make choices that will lead to more positive and productive outcomes. It also includes a success action planer and a reading group guide.

Success Starts Now: Timeless Principles To Help You Win.

If you're ready to take your life to the next level and accelerate your success this book will help you map out a plan to get from where you are now to where you want to be.

> ➤ To order Cassandra Mack's books go to:
> **StrategiesForEmpoweredLiving.com**

If You Enjoyed This Book
Leave A Review On Amazon

If you enjoyed this book or received value from it in any way, then I'd like to ask you for a favor: would you be kind enough to leave a review for this book on Amazon? It'd be greatly appreciated! Your Amazon reviews help to get this book into more hands that need to hear this message. Thank you.

Made in the USA
San Bernardino, CA
28 November 2018